A Guide to
Philosophy
in Six Hours
and Fifteen
Minutes

A Guide to

Philosophy

in Six Hours

and Fifteen

Minutes

Witold Gombrowicz

Translated by Benjamin Ivry

Yale University Press

New Haven and London

Published with assistance from the Louis Stern
Memorial Fund.

Designed by Nancy Ovedovitz and set in Adobe
Garamond type by Integrated Publishing Solutions.
Printed in the United States of America
by R. R. Donnelley.

Library of Congress Cataloging-in-Publication Data
Gombrowicz, Witold.
[Cours de philosophie en six heures un quart. English]
A guide to philosophy in six hours and fifteen minutes /
Witold Gombrowicz ; translated by Benjamin Ivry.

p.   cm.

ISBN 0-300-10409-X (cloth : alk. paper)
1. Philosophy, European.   2. Philosophy, Modern.
I. Ivry, Benjamin.   II. Title.
B792.G6513   2004
190—dc22   2004005687

A catalogue record for this book is available from the
British Library.

The paper in this book meets the guidelines for
permanence and durability of the Committee on
Production Guidelines for Book Longevity of the
Council on Library Resources.

10 9 8 7 6 5 4 3 2 1

A Guide to
Philosophy
in Six Hours
and Fifteen
Minutes

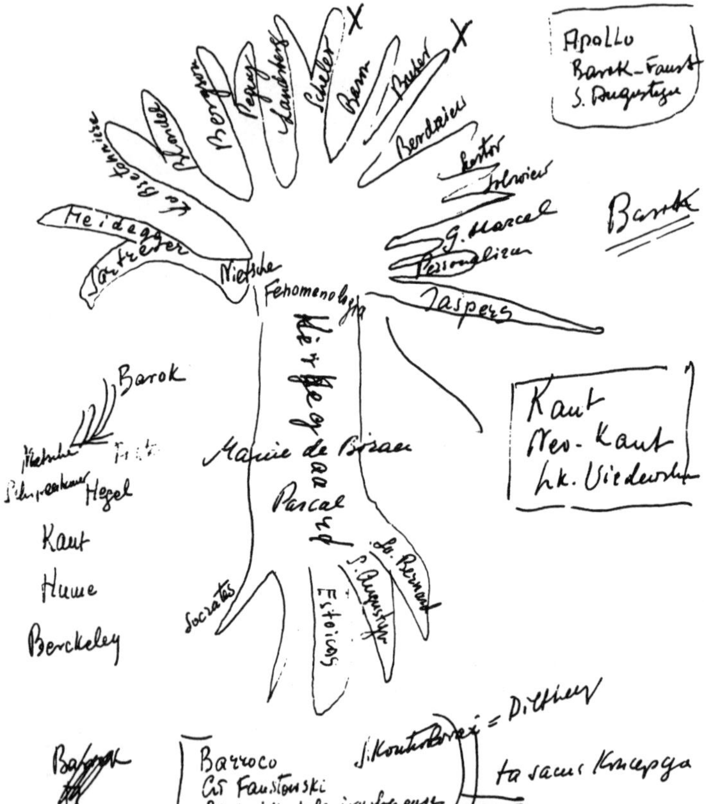
Apollo
Barok-Faust
Barok
Heidegger
Sartre
Nietsche
Fenomenologia
Scheler
Buber
Berdiajew
G. Marcel
Jaspers
Kierkegaard
Marie de Biran
Pascal
Socrates
Estoicos
Kant
Neo-Kant
Barok
Hegel
Kant
Hume
Berckeley
Barroco
= Dilthey
ta sama koncepcja

First Lesson

Sunday, April 27, 1969
*Referendum**

Kant 1724–1804

Beginning of modern thought.

One could also say that this is *Descartes* (beginning of the 17th century).

Descartes: a single important idea: *absolute doubt.*

Here rationalism begins: subject everything to absolute doubt, until the moment when reason forces us to accept an idea.

(Basis for the phenomenology of Husserl)

—subject: thinking self

—object: opera glasses—table

—the idea of an object which forms in my consciousness.

*A popular referendum on April 27, 1969, offered French voters a variety of proposed administrative reforms. When President Charles de Gaulle received an unexpected defeat in the vote, he resigned the presidency the following day and went into retirement. [Translator's note.]

Descartes reduces these three aspects of knowledge.

I am certain that this is in my consciousness but does not correspond to reality. For example, the centaur.

Systematic doubt. Puts the world in doubt, in parentheses:

1. the object.

2. everything involving the object.

The only certainty is that they exist *in my consciousness.*

In parentheses:

the idea of God;

the sciences which relate to reality (supposedly objective): sociology, psychology, except for the abstract sciences; mathematics and logic, because they do not concern the outside world, but are laws for my own consciousness.

What is Descartes' great error, "deviation" (to use Husserl's term)? *Descartes feared the terrifying consequences* of his ideas. He tries to show the objective reality of God—and therefore of the world (as God's creation).

Descartes' fear is similar to that of Sartre. Because of it, all his later philosophy was distorted. For Descartes, the important thing is *Discourse on the Method*. TO ELIMINATE THE OBJECT: Descartes' great idea.

Philosophy begins to deal with consciousness as something fundamental. Imagine an absolute night, with a single object. If this object does not encounter a consciousness capable of sensing its existence, then it does not exist.

There is no individual consciousness, but *consciousness* in general.

(The brain's consciousness, etc.)

The dog.

Descartes, precursor of modern thought.

Kant

Berkeley (rural youth)

Hume.

Kant

Newton, especially.

Descartes.

Kant is based on rational knowledge, organized scientifically. Influenced by Newton.

Works: *Critique of Pure Reason; Critique of Practical Reason*

Kant's big thing: *Critique of Pure Reason.*

It is not about a critique of pure reason; we want to judge our own consciousness. *Consciousness judged by consciousness.* Example: can we be sure of the existence of God through philosophical deduction?

Questions: to what extent can one be sure about consciousness? To what extent can consciousness be authentic?

Kant's reasoning in the *Critique of Pure Reason,* even expressed obscurely, is:

Everything that we know about the world is expressed in judgments.

For example, "I exist," and a conditional judgment, "If I kick Dominique,* he'll kick me twice."

This is the connection of causality.

Judgments are analytical or synthetic.

Analytical judgments are those which derive from analysis, dissecting a whole into its significant parts. Kant says that analytical judgments add nothing to our knowledge because they underscore an element of their definition.

*Dominique de Roux. [Except as otherwise specified, all notes appeared in the original French edition. —Ed.]

Example, the definition of man: living being, mammal, etc. Take the notion "living": "man is a living being." Why? Because there is decomposition. It is a concept drawn from another concept, in other words, an element drawn from the definition.

Synthetic judgments. A different approach: adding something. Therefore they enrich our knowledge of the world.

Synthetic judgments have no *a priori* value (*a priori:* independent of any experience).

Synthetic judgments are *a posteriori,* in other words, based on experience.

Example: water boils when it reaches a certain degree of heat.

Enrichment of our knowledge. New phenomenon in our understanding of the world.

A posteriori judgments are not always accurate. Example: there is no guarantee that water will begin to boil again on the 10,000th try.

Kant seeks precision. He grips reality. A solid mind.

Nevertheless, there are some synthetic judgments which are *a priori,* which add something to reality, but at the same time one is convinced of their infallibility. Newton's influence.

Example: the action is equivalent to the re-action.

From the moment that we discovered this, we are certain that *it will always be that way.*

Example: the shortest distance between two points is a straight line.

Yet for Einstein, the shortest distance between two points is a curved line. But that does not change anything, because it is a different reality from that of Newton. If you accept all of Newton's premises, then Newton's laws are absolute in the context of his reality.

Some synthetic judgments are:

A priori—which increase our knowledge—and which are absolute and valid for all of humanity.

The whole problem of Kantian philosophy thus resides in a single question: how are *a priori* synthetic judgments possible?

Kant asks this question because such judgments, without being accidental or based on experience, nevertheless enrich our knowledge, without being accidental or based on experience. Synthetic —which provides an eternal novelty.

Kant proceeds with
three analyses

three sections of the *Critique of Pure Reason.*

But since the subject is reason, or organized knowledge, everything must be based on synthetic knowledge.

It is science which formulates *synthetic, a priori* judgments (that is, eternal).

First part: Transcendental Aesthetics.

(Transcendent means something outside of the self).

Aesthetics used in the mathematical sense.

Mathematics: science of forms and relationships.

In this first part: How are synthetic *a priori* judgments possible in mathematics?

Second part: Transcendental Analytics.

We treat judgments in *physics.* Everything that we know about the subject of things (behavior, reactions). All that is the object of physics.

It is the science of things.

Third part: Transcendental Dialectics, where he deals with metaphysical problems such as that of the "existence of God."

With Kant begins the great reduction of thought, a process which lasts to the present day.

For the first time consciousness asks the question: *What are the limits of consciousness* (of reason)?

Kant's great coup. He had some stunning ideas that completely changed everything.

Question: How are *a priori synthetic judgments* possible?

Answer: A priori synthetic judgments are possible in general and therefore in transcendental aesthetics, *because time and space are not a property of things but rather a property of the subject.*

In order for something to exist for us, we must inject it with time and space.

And here Kantian reasoning is simple.

He says, "There are three reasons why space does not exist in the objective world outside us, but is an integral part of our consciousness."

First argument. Space does not come from an experience, *but is the inevitable condition of all experience.* Space is not an object but the condition of the existence of the object. Space does not derive from experience.

Second argument. Space is not a concept obtained by deduction. We cannot understand it as concrete, because it is not an object. Space is pure intuition. In other words, space is not a thing but the condition of a thing, because we possess it within ourselves.

Third argument (or rather, consequence). The intuition of space is the inevitable condition of our *a priori* synthetic judgments, conferring objective reality on things.

Without it, these are merely impressions (parallel to Descartes).

Example: geometry, resting on constructions in space, on figures, is not based on experience but valid because [*sentence incomplete in the text*].*

Conclusion

We have demonstrated that Kant's *a priori* synthetic judgments are in fact *analytical judgments.*

This splendid construction collapses.

And Kant's idea of the categories of pure reason will collapse as well.

That is the fate of all philosophy. No system endures. Through philosophy, human consciousness in progress discovers itself for itself, as Hegel will say so magnificently.

---

*Bracketed indications of gaps in the text appear in the French edition. [Editor's note.]

—There is no point in asking whether one should do philosophy or not. We do philosophy because we must. It is inevitable. Our consciousness asks us questions and we must try to resolve them. Philosophy is a necessary thing.

What was the most profound vision of the world in the 18th century? One finds it in Kant, without whom it would be impossible to know the development of consciousness through the centuries. Philosophy is needed for a global view of culture. It is important for writers.

Philosophy allows us to organize culture, to introduce order, to find ourselves, and to attain intellectual confidence.

Second Lesson

Monday, April 28, 1969

Kant: The Categories

Two elements do not belong to external reality, but are injected by us into the object: space and time.

Space is not an object, but the condition for every possible object.

The reasoning is the same for time.

Time is not a thing that can be tested, but all things are *in* time.

One can very well imagine time without phenomena, but it is impossible to imagine a phenomenon without time.

Same argument for space.

One cannot imagine different time (like objects: table, chair). Time is always the same. It does not derive from our observation of the external world but is a direct intuition, an intuitive knowledge, that is, an immediate knowledge.

We need to add that time permits *a priori* synthetic judgments in arithmetic. The impressions that we have of the external world follow each other in succession; this is what arithmetic is about: 1-2-3-4. It is a sequence.

A priori synthetic judgments are confirmed in experience because they are carried out in time. In the same way, all judgments related to mathematics are *a priori* synthetic judgments, confirmed by experience.

Transcendental Analysis

Transcendental analysis takes the physical sciences as its object, since physics unites everything that we know about the world.

I repeat: Kant does not speak much about consciousness, but rather about pure reason.

Why?

Because it involves an organized, rational knowledge, which appears in science. Here we arrive at a very beautiful Kantian inspiration which resembles the Copernican revolution. Just as Copernicus immobilized the sun and made the earth move, Kant demonstrates that *only the co-relativity of subject and object can form a reality.* The object must be seized by consciousness in order to form reality in time and space. In physics (Newton), we have direct knowledge about *a priori* things.

Example, we can affirm forever (absolute) that all phenomena are subject to the law of causality and Newton's famous law that action equals reaction, for instance [*sentence incomplete*].

Once again: how can *a priori* synthetic judgments be possible in physics?

Kant's great coup: our knowledge pertaining to such things is expressed *by judgments.*

Kant took up the classification of judgments according to Aristotelian logic (which was valid in Kant's day).

Aristotle's judgments can be classified by the following criteria:

1. *Quantity.* Example: individual judgments which relate to a single phenomenon. But if you make a judgment like: certain men are white, then you express a particular judgment.

One can also express as judgment that all men are mortal.

2. *Quality.* Affirmative judgments A.

negative ones B.

infinitive ones C.

(which lead to an infinite judgment: example, fish are not birds).

Kant's discovery consists in deducing—in eliciting—*a category* from each of these judgments.

Example: A. affirmative judgment: "You are French."

(category: UNITY).

B. particular judgment: "Certain men are mortal."

(category of MULTIPLE)

C. universal judgment: "All men are mortal."

(category of the set: TOTALITY).

Consciousness is the fundamental thing.

Object-subject: nothing more.

1. consciousness cannot be a mechanism, nor broken up into parts, because it has no parts. It is a whole.

2. consciousness cannot be conditioned by science. It is what permits science, but science cannot explain something to us about consciousness.

Consciousness is not the brain, nor the body, because I am conscious of my brain, but the brain cannot be conscious.

TAKE CARE not to imagine consciousness as an organism or an animal.

There is an important boundary between science and philosophy. Science establishes its methods, its laws by experience. But it is valid only in the world of phenomena. Science can give us the connection between things, but not direct knowledge about the essence of things.

In appearance, there is a contradiction, because if consciousness is the basic element, how can it have categories? How can one divide it like a scientifically analyzed mechanism?

Categories, judgments, cannot belong to consciousness.

In the Kantian corpus, consciousness judges itself. Kant's fundamental problem is: *How is our knowledge of the world possible?* It is precisely our consciousness that realizes the limits of our consciousness. Here one could imagine that one takes a step back to form another consciousness, which judges the first. In that case a third consciousness must judge the second one, etc. (Husserl).

But consciousness cannot be a judge. Consciousness (following Alain's definition) means *knowing what one knows,* and nothing more. Even this definition is bad, because it divides consciousness. Consciousness is indivisible and unconditional. To tell the truth, in philosophy, one cannot say anything.

What are Kant's categories?

Are these the conditions that make consciousness possible?

In Kant (as I see it) there is this process: consciousness is judged from a distance by another consciousness. It is merely a question of establishing what the conditions of this first consciousness are for the second.

It is only a matter of knowing what the indispensable conditions for this second consciousness are, in order that the first consciousness may be thought about without its elements. Consciousness is impossible for us to imagine.

Kantian categories are the condition for a subject to be conscious of an object. But these conditions cannot have an absolute sense. Categories seem to us like the condition for every judgment about reality.

It must be said (as with time) that the categories are within us. It is we who can capture reality by injecting categories.

Nothing has remained of Kant's fine theories, not even the most important category which comes from conditional judgment (hypothetical), for example:

if I . . .

therefore I . . .

did not stay.

But now philosophy deals with other things. These were formal discoveries, but significant ones, because they absolutely revolutionized the notion of consciousness, of the subject-object connection, thus of man and the universe.

Third Lesson

April 30, 1969

Kant

Third part of the *Critique of Pure Reason.*
Possibility of synthetic judgments . . . .

. . . .

metaphysical

Metaphysical: everything which is not physical, like the soul, the world, and God.

These three components are not direct perceptions (like a chair) but syntheses. Yet the soul is the
synthesis of all impressions, because it is man's self
(the soul) which assimilates all impressions. The
soul is that which receives the perceptions.

The second synthesis, that is, that of the
world, is the synthesis of everything. Yet the critique
of the idea of the soul consists in demonstrating that
all our perceptions are in time, while the soul is not
in time. The soul is immortal.

Then Kant moves to the idea of the Cosmos,
that is, of the world. He shows that there are four
antinomies of pure reason, which exclude each other.

First antinomy. The world has a beginning in time and limits in space. This has no meaning, because when the collective world (of things) finishes, we still have space and time. But as the world is the synthesis of everything, it cannot be limited to a limited whole. One must see here a certain philosophical idea which consists of reducing things to obvious facts.

Second antinomy. The cosmos is made up simultaneously of divisible and indivisible elements. One can reduce this antinomy to what could be called the limitation of the thing. The thing (or object) must inevitably be limited in order for it to be a thing. That is why time and space cannot be considered things. Yet the concept of thing, in order to reach fullness, must inevitably insert time and space, since the Cosmos signifies absolutely everything that exists. We see a contradiction here, since the Cosmos must be unlimited in time and space in order to include absolutely everything. It is this way when you take an object; you can divide it endlessly. There are no limits for it. The idea of an object therefore contains a contradiction because it must be limited and unlimited at the same time.

Third antinomy of the idea of the Cosmos. For

us, the Cosmos must have a cause because [*sentence incomplete*] internally contradictory idea.

Fourth antinomy. God must exist for *us,* and at the same time he *cannot exist.* Kant lists three theological arguments here to demonstrate the existence of God. Now, [*sentence incomplete*].

First argument: ontological. Ontological means everything that concerns the being. We have an idea of God as a perfect being. But a perfect being, to have perfection, must also have the quality of *existing.* This argument seems too sophisticated to me. Kant says that the category of existence is a perception. Yet God cannot be perceived.

Second argument: cosmological. The world must have a cause since, according to the category of causality, each thing must have a cause. If this is so, God must also have a cause.

Third argument: teleological. Telos means *purpose.* Everything that is in the world must have a purpose, must be the work of God. But if God is teleological, then he himself should be created for an end.

Kant emphasizes that the errors of metaphysics originate in what it implements beyond the limits of experience and its use of categories.

We arrive at the last thesis of the *Critique of Pure Reason.* Kant demonstrates that our reason is not sufficient to discover what he calls the *noumenon.** For example, if you see an object, you have the impression that it is a white object made in a certain way, etc. But if you just put on yellow-tinted glasses, everything changes. Imagine an ant that looks at the same object and sees it only in two dimensions and not three. Now, whether for an ant or for a person donning yellow-tinted glasses, the object will change.

Kant wonders whether pure reason can discover the *object in itself,* objectively, independently of our ways of perceiving it. He notices that this is impossible, and we can never know what the *noumenon, the absolute,* is in itself, independent of our own perceptions. We are limited to the phenomenological world. This is important, because you will find this problem in Husserl, Hegel, etc. Our reason must be limited to the phenomenological world.

The *phenomenon* is what I see according to my faculties, and my way of seeing things: Psina,† for

*Gombrowicz uses the term *numen,* hereafter translated as *noumenon,* −a. [Translator's note.]
†Psina, Gombrowicz's little dog.

me, is white, in time and space. That is the phenomenon. The *noumenon* (the absolute) consists in asking oneself, "How is Psina, not for me, but *in itself?*" The Kantian critique is a *limitation of thought.* Human thinking would consider itself capable of understanding everything. But since Kant, not to mention Descartes, thinking has undergone a reduction and this reduction is extremely important. It demonstrates that thinking reaches a certain maturity, it begins to know its limits, and you will find in all later philosophy, for example, in Feuerbach, in Husserl, in Marx, etc., the same tendency to reduce thought. Today philosophy does not consist of seeking an absolute truth, like the existence of God, but is more limited, limiting itself only to the phenomenological world, where it replaces the question, "What is the world?" with "How to change the world?" (Marx) and it finds the purest expression in the phenomenological method of Husserl, who is not at all interested in the *noumena,* but in phenomena.

Critique of Practical Reason, Kant's second great work.

Today this work is outdated, although it has very authentic passages. Kant wanted to make of it something akin to the *Critique of Pure Reason.* But if the *Critique of Pure Reason* speaks about judgments by which one can know the world, the *Critique of Practical Reason* deals with judgments which *qualify things* (the quality of things). Example: this man pleases me, this bread is good.

Here we perceive judgments as imperative judgments.

Critique of Pure Reason: it is about understanding, about knowing.

Critique of Practical Reason: it is about what I must do, to act (morals).

Now, imperatives can be hypothetical or categorical.

Imperatives when the will is autonomous, conditioned by nothing. Example: "One must be moral" is categorical. It does not depend on any condition. If I say that I must be moral in order to go to heaven or to have people's respect, this is already a hypothetical imperative. This is important because, in our era, we confuse these things.

For Kant, the moral imperative must be disinterested.

Now morality depends entirely on will. Be careful: these are Kantian laws which are interpreted in a confused way. Example: if my mother is ill and I, with the best intentions of curing her, by mistake give her medicine which kills her, from the moral point of view, I am in order.

That is why one must judge all of history's greatest monsters by their *intentions:* Hitler, Stalin.

If Hitler believed that the Jews were the malady of the world, he was in order from a moral point of view, even though he was wrong. But if he did so out of personal interest, then it is immoral. Morality, for him, is moral will, goodwill.

Aristotle,   this is classification, order,
            the objective world.
            Man considered as object, animal.

Marx.   For Marx, man is object.

[Witold disagrees]. The artist must be in the subjective.

Read Kant's biography by Thomas de Quincey.

Fourth Lesson

Thursday, May 1, 1969

Schopenhauer

After Kant, there is a line of thought which could be outlined as follows:

Fichte

Schelling German Idealism

Hegel

"Idealism" why? Because it is subjective philosophy which is concerned with ideas.

Kant had two successors (curious thing) of two different types:

Schopenhauer

Nietzsche

Arthur Schopenhauer (19th century).

Born in Danzig.

He adopts the Kantian system with a formidable difference, which consists of the following.

After Kant, all philosophers wanted to be involved with the thing in itself, the absolute. Yet Schopenhauer gets up and says, "It so happens that no one knows what a thing is in itself, and well, me, I do know."

The world is stupefied, and Schopenhauer continues: "I know it from internal intuition." Intuition means direct knowledge, not reasoned but "absolute."

Schopenhauer's reasoning is as follows.

Man is also a thing. Therefore, if I myself am a thing, I must seek my absolute in my intuition, what I am in my essence. And, says Schopenhauer, "I know that the most elementary and fundamental thing in myself is the will to live."

Here a door opens to a new philosophical thinking: philosophy stops being an intellectual demonstration, in order to enter into direct contact with life. For me (in France, almost no one shares my opinion) it is an extremely important date that opens the path to Nietzsche's will to power, and to all of existential philosophy. We must understand that Schopenhauer's metaphysical system did not take hold; in this sense, Schopenhauer did not express something solid. Which is why, I suppose, that Schopenhauer has not held his own as a philosopher.

BUT WHAT IS PHILOSOPHY? No philosophical system lasts for very long. But for me, philosophy has

THE SUPREME VALUE OF ORGANIZING THE WORLD IN A VISION.

For example, there are the extremely grandiose Kantian and Hegelian universes, there is also Nietzsche's, and it is there where Schopenhauer is important.

Let us move from this vision of Schopenhauer to the Schopenhauerian world.

This is the first time that philosophy touches life.

What is the will to live for Schopenhauer?

He himself says that he uses these words because nothing better comes to mind. In truth, it is more the will to be, because for Schopenhauer, not only do man and animals want to live, but also the rock that resists and the light that persists. Schopenhauer says that this is the Kantian *noumenon,* this is the absolute.

IMPORTANT For Schopenhauer, in the metaphysical sense (beyond physical), this concerns a single will to be, absolutely identical for me and for this table.

This will to live, in order to be seen as phenomenon, must assume [*sentence incomplete*].

It must exist in space and time, in the numerical order of things. It is a single entity, because the numerical world knows neither time nor object, nor anything of the kind.

But when this will to live passes to the phenomenological world, becoming a phenomenon limited by time and space, then it inevitably becomes divided. By the effect of a law that Schopenhauer called *principium individuationis,* it becomes individual, specific. I repeat: Kant demonstrated that we can never penetrate the world of *noumena;* for instance, it is impossible, with reasoning, to prove the existence of God. In this sense, Kant said that our reasoning is limited to the phenomenological world. Time and space are not beyond us, it is the thinking subject which introduces them into the world, therefore we cannot perceive anything infinite, universal like God.

It is only in time and space that the *noumenon* can manifest itself as phenomenon. It is for this reason that Schopenhauer says that the *will to live is a noumenon.* It is beyond time and space, it is within itself and can manifest itself only when it becomes a phenomenon (limited in time and space).

When the will to live is manifested in the phenomenological world, it is divided into a countless number of things that consume one another in order to live. The wolf feeds on the cat, the cat on the mouse, etc.

Schopenhauer's great merit is to have found that decisive thing: death, pain, the eternal war that each being must wage in order to survive.

I always considered that philosophy must not be intellectual but something which starts from our sensibility. For example, for me, the simple fact that I am aware of the existence of a tree has no importance until it brings me pleasure or pain. Only then does it become significant. It is this idea which I try to introduce in interviews, etc.

We are in an absolutely tragic world. They say that Schopenhauer is pessimistic. That is not saying very much. It is a grandiose and tragic vision which, unfortunately, coincides perfectly with reality. Schopenhauer deduces several conclusions from his system.

For example, nature is not concerned only with individuals but with the species. Millions of ants must die in order to generate the species. Likewise, if a man sacrifices himself in a battle, it is also for the same reason. Finally, Schopenhauer was a raging misogynist for the very simple reason that women are involved with the continuation of the species. He said that in love as well, personal happiness cannot exist because the individual is sacrificed for the species. It is very moving, that attentive way in which a young man looks at a young girl, and *vice versa.* They only want to know whether they can have children "of good quality."

We look for our opposites in the opposite sex: big nose, small nose, etc. Man can never attain individual happiness. Our will to live forces us to consume others or to be consumed by them. As a result, Schopenhauer analyzes various noble feelings (example: the woman's love for the child); he demonstrates that all that goes against individual happiness. After that, he likewise shows that what one calls happiness or pleasure is nothing more than the satisfying of a malaise. If you enjoy eating steak, it is because you felt hungry beforehand.

For Schopenhauer, life is a continuous, culpable malaise.

According to Schopenhauer, what possibility is there of leaving this hellish *imbroglio?*

Suicide? No, this would be useless because by committing suicide, we only confirm our will to live. Because if I kill myself, it is because my will to live was not satisfied.

The sole way of breaking free of the will to live is by renunciation.

I kill my will to live within myself.

This is what led Schopenhauer to Hindu philosophy and Eastern philosophy, which is exactly what promulgates meditation and the renunciation of life.

It must be said that this thesis is rather artificial and that the part of his work devoted to eastern philosophy, on the *World as Will and Representation,* is the least convincing.

Fifth Lesson

Friday, May 2, 1969

Schopenhauer recognizes two possibilities:

1. To affirm the will to live by fully participating in life with its cruelties and its injustices.

2. Not suicide, but *meditation.*

Schopenhauer considers that the contemplation of the world "as if it were a game" is absolutely superior to life. He demonstrates this in an extremely ingenious way. The one who contemplates the world and is filled with wonder is the artist. Now, in this sense, the artist resembles a child, because the child also marvels at the world in a disinterested way. It is for this reason, says Schopenhauer, that children are brilliant, simply because they are children. During our first few years, we make more progress than during the rest of our life. That is why, in the East, the yogi (the one who meditates) attains the unique possibility of suppressing life.

Schopenhauer formulates an artistic theory which, for me, is the most important of all. And, just between us, the extremely naïve and incomplete manner of dealing with art in France is due primarily to the ignorance of Schopenhauer.

Art shows us nature's game and its forces, namely the will to live. Schopenhauer is *concrete* in this matter. He asks: why does the façade of a cathedral charm us, when a simple wall does not interest us? It is because the will to live of matter is expressed in weight and resistance. Now, a wall does not display the game of these forces, since each particle of the wall both resists and carries weight. While a cathedral façade shows these forces in action, since the columns resist and the capitals press down. We see the struggle between weight and resistance. He also explains to us why a twisted (curved) column does not satisfy us. Quite simply because it does not resist enough. In the same way, a rounded column is better than a square column.

All this to tell you how Schopenhauer sees ART.

It is meditation that he sets in opposition to life.

He also deals with *sculpture* and says that the beauty of man derives from *a priori* anticipation based on experience. The human body is all the more successful since it is well adapted to its ends. He adds that there is within us an ideal of human beauty, which consists of prolonging in the future what we consider to be of quality today, such as long legs. This quality always obliges man to go further in this direction, health, etc. One could say that this is a kind of dream about the design of the species in the future.

For Schopenhauer, the beauty of *Greek sculp-ture* consisted in a discernment between sexual instinct and beauty. In a word, Greek beauty is not exciting, and that is why it is superior.

Painting. If sculpture is primarily concerned with beauty and charm, painting seeks expression, passion, and character in man. Therefore, in painting one can also consider the ugly to be handsome. Example: an old woman. Character unifies a person in painting, because character is what unifies in a sense (direction); if not, man would be disparate.

Literature. The artist, in general, does not function by concepts of logic, of abstractions, but has direct intuition of the will to live in the world.

For this reason, Schopenhauer notes that discursive literature which tries to prove something is useless. One cannot make art with abstract principles, with concepts. If I have something to say about a subject, for example, about illegitimate children, I shall simply say it in a lecture and not in a work of art.

The work of art seeks the concrete, but in the concrete, it rediscovers the universal, the will to live. Think of the miser in Molière. He is a concrete character who has a life, a hair color, etc., but through him we can see avarice in its universal sense. Schopenhauer gives the definition of the genius, which is still very close to that of the child. *The genius is disinterested.* He has fun with the world. He perceives its atrocities but delights in its atrocities. The genius in general is useless in practical life, because he does not seek his personal interest. He is antisocial, but sees the world better because he is *objective.*

Schopenhauer makes a very good comparison in saying that a mediocre man's intelligence resembles a flashlight, which shines only on what it is seeking, whereas a superior intelligence is like the sun, which illuminates everything. From there derives *the objectivity of the art of the genius.* It is *disinterested.*

Schopenhauer said much on the subject of genius, for example that the genius cannot live normally; the artist always has an obstacle which prevents him from living: illness, abnormality, infirmity, homosexuality, etc.

(Intelligent men are highly sensitive to noise). Me, personally, I interpret this by the fact that *we sense better what we lack.* Example: a cavalry officer does not even realize that he is healthy, whereas an invalid like Chopin has an acute notion of health, because he lacks it.

One can observe phenomena like Beethoven who, personally, was hysterical and unhappy, yet in his art so well expressed health, balance (no doubt because he lacked these).

Myself, I attach the highest importance to *antinomy in art*. An artist must be that and its opposite. Mad, disorganized but also disciplined, cold, rigorous. Art is never a single thing, but is always compensated by its opposite.

Schopenhauer is not really philosophy, but rather intuitiveness and morality. He was outraged that on a Pacific island each year, sea tortoises emerge from the water to procreate on the beach, where they are flipped over and devoured by the island's wild dogs. He said, "This is life, this is what has been systematically repeated for millennia, each spring."

Why don't we read more Schopenhauer?

Why isn't he current?

1. Schopenhauer's metaphysics (first part of the book) is not valid today (I know that *noumenon* is intuition, the will to live), formulated in this way.

2. No doubt the *aristocratic aspect* of this philosophy. For Schopenhauer, there are mediocre men and superior men. He insulted the mediocre ones.

3. He was against life (his philosophy was against it), whereas one can derive some very useful things about politics from Hegel, as Marx did.

Schopenhauer sought renunciation, he sought to kill the will to live.

For me, it is a mystery that interesting books like Schopenhauer's (and my own!) do not find readers.

Schopenhauer detested Hegel. He always said "that oaf, Hegel!" To defy Hegel, he had set the times of his courses at the University of Berlin to be the same as Hegel's, with the result that Hegel's classroom was always full while his own was empty.

But Hegel and Schopenhauer had arguments to show why a genius cannot be successful, because he surpasses his own time. That is why genius is incomprehensible and serves no one. Yet Schopenhauer and I console ourselves rather well!

Sixth Lesson

Saturday, May 3

Hegel

Dull biography. 19th century. Professor in Berlin.

Kant

Fichte: Philosophy of the State and of law.

Schelling: Artistic nature. His philosophy is much influenced by aesthetics and art. Hegel attacked him violently.

Hegel's fundamental thesis is: *what is rational is real, and what is real is rational.*

This is not so difficult. The main idea is that the subject is correlative with (dependent on) the object, that one cannot exist without the other.

Imagine that only one thing exists. If there is no consciousness, this thing does not exist. It is on this basis that Hegel formulates his *theory of the real.*

The world is a thing, it is understood to the extent that it is assimilated by reason, by a rational consciousness. Hegel gives a grandiose image of this process.

Let us imagine that I entered a cathedral. At first I see nothing more than the entrance, fragments of walls, architectural details which are not self-explanatory. In short, I see the cathedral in a fragmentary way. I advance. As I advance, the more I see the cathedral and finally I reach the other end and I see it in its entirety. I discover the meaning of each fragment. The cathedral penetrated my REASON; IT IS. This is exactly the process of our development in the world. Each day, we understand the world better, we are better aware of the reason for every phenomenon. Thus each time the world exists a little more for us. There will come a moment, the final moment of our history and of the human race, where the world will be fully assimilated. On that day, time and space will disappear and the conjunction of subject and object will be transformed into an *absolute.* Beyond time and space. There will no longer be any movement. Then poof! the ABSOLUTE.

As you see, such metaphysical systems have a rather fantastic structure. Even when the systems collapse, they are useful in understanding reality and the world a little better. This idea of the progress of reason in Hegel is achieved through a dialectical system which is of the greatest importance today and which expresses itself somewhat this way.

Each thesis finds its antithesis at a higher degree. This synthesis appears anew as a thesis and finds its antinomy, etc. Thus this is a law of development based on contradiction. According to Hegel, our mind is based on this contradiction because it is imperfect, because it knows reality only partially. Thus its judgments are imperfect.

Hegel discovers this contradiction in the very foundation of the mind; for example, when we say *all,* we must accept the *singular.* When we imagine something *black,* we must also think of another *color* because the very idea of color is an opposition between it and all the other colors. The same opposition can be found in the historical development of the State.

For example, a dictatorship provokes a revolution, and a revolution encounters its synthesis in a system which is neither that of the dictatorship nor of the revolution, a system thus of limited power which, in turn, finds correction in a system, for example oligarchic.

Or when you think *all,* you are obliged to think *nothing,* and it is this way that one advances, step by step, inside that cathedral.

Hegel's philosophy is a *philosophy of becoming,* which is a great step ahead, since this process of becoming does not appear in earlier philosophies. It is not only a movement, but a progression, since this dialectical process always puts us on a higher rung, until the final outcome of reason, and in Hegel, this process is naturally based on the progress of reason, that is, of science. Which leads him to give the greatest importance to *history.*

For Hegel, nature is not creative. It does not advance. The sun, for example, always rises and sets the same way. But what is creative is *human evolution,* which expresses itself especially in history. Already one can notice great chasms which open in the mind between what is now called

synchronic

and diachronic.

This abyss is part of the great contradictions that always characterize the human mind, like, for example, the subject-object or Einstein's theory of a space-time continuum, Planck's quantum theory or the way of detecting the electron, or in the corpuscular and undulatory theory of light.* In this per-

---

*In this passage, *corpusculaire* and *ondulatoire,* respectively, refer to "particles" and "waves," properties of light in physics. [Translator's note.]

spective, the human mind seems like something created by two different elements which never meet each other.

Man is precisely this *hole*.

Again a formula from Hegel which will give you an idea of his rather complicated language: man is the principle through which the world's reason arrives at *self-awareness*.

Let us now take a look at Hegel's logic. It is presented *grosso modo* in the following way:

I assert that nothing exists, but because I assert it, then at least my assertion exists. Therefore the being exists (in opposition to the thing). But since the being in itself signifies nothing, in saying *being*, I must say that something is. By this path, I come to recognize that the category of the being may be thought about only with that of the non-being; what I already told you in speaking about the mind's antinomy. But I simply want to show what is the starting point for this logic.

The difference between traditional logic and Hegel's is this: according to traditional logic, everything that is, is identical to itself and nothing contradicts itself. This is just the well-known *identity principle* by which A is equivalent to A.

But in Hegel, nothing is identical to itself and everything contradicts itself. (The imperfection of reason in operation: as long as I have not entirely seen the cathedral, the sense is imperfect. A equals A is not achieved here.)

This leads to what I announced at the beginning: it is *thought* which is the basis of reality. We need only compare the Hegelian world to the world of Aristotle or Saint Thomas to understand that the Hegelian world is truth in progress, where humanity devises its own laws and man becomes a rung in history.

The importance which Hegel attributed to history surely contributed to the triumph of Hegel's thought.

In order to give you a more detailed idea of this thinking, which will show you to what extent my abbreviations are far from containing a complete picture, I would like to speak to you about an important book by Hegel, *The Phenomenology of Mind,* vol. II.

Chapter six (in order to show the path of his thought). The truly ethical mind is divided into two parts: the ethical world, the human and divine world and man and woman.

This is subdivided into:

1. Nation and family. The law of day and the law of night,

which is subdivided again into

A. human law

B. divine law

C. the rights of the individual.

2. The movement that one finds in both laws (always becoming):

A. government—wars—negative power

B. (very important). The ethical relationship between man and woman in the sense of brother and sister.

C. The reciprocal influence of divine and human law.

3. The epic world as being an infinite thing, therefore a totality.

The Hegelian analysis of these themes always consists of discovering and defining the dialectical movement to which they are subject. This leads him to truly astonishing results, to famous passages like the one on the dialectics between master and slave.

I have not yet spoken about an extremely important theme for Hegel, *State* and *peoples* (nations).

For Hegel, the reality of the State is superior to that of the individual. For him, the State is the incarnation of the Mind in the world. Here are some definitions which permit us to understand his notion of the State.

(The State is the reality of the moral idea. It is the moral mind as will (intention), self-evident and substantial, which thinks by itself and *knows* and realizes what it knows as knowledge.)

This horrible sentence shows the most profound sense of the Hegelian idea, which can be expressed in the following very superficial way: for earlier philosophy, man was subject to a moral law instituted by God or, as in Kant, subject to a moral imperative. In other words, man functions but the law already exists. But in Hegel, everything moves. In advancing, man crafts his own law, and there is no fixed law beyond that which is constituted by the dialectical process. In Hegel, not only man but laws are in progress because they are imperfect.

Again, two definitions of the State in Hegel.

1. The State is the realization of individual will.

2. The State is the mind which blossoms in becoming the world's form and organization.

Next he analyzes various forms of government. And he submits it to the dialectical process: the capitalist government provokes an opposing dictatorship, that of the proletariat. The dictatorship of the proletariat leads to a superior form which will know how to combine the good points of each previous form, etc.

Thesis—antithesis—synthesis.

You understand how greedily *the Communists* threw themselves on this idea. For them, revolution leads to a dictatorship of the proletariat, but afterward one arrives at the ideal State, which has nothing to do with strength.

Hegel owes his glory first to Marx, and secondly to the Marxists.

War, for Hegel, is also a dialectical process in which the immoral leads to the moral.

Finally, the State transforms itself into the incarnation of the divinity.

Hegel/Kierkegaard
Kierkegaard's Attack

This is the last great metaphysical system to be formed. According to dialectical law in pure Hegelian style, the thesis meets its antithesis, and Kierkegaard is the antithesis.

Kierkegaard was a Danish pastor, a great admirer of Hegel. Suddenly he declared war on him, in one of culture's most dramatic moments.

The following summarizes Kierkegaard's attack on Hegel:

Hegel is absolutely irreproachable in his theory, but this *theory is worthless.*

And why?

Because it is abstract, while *existence* (it is the first time that this word appears) is concrete.

In Hegel there are only abstractions and concepts; for example, I saw a thousand horses that all have something in common, and thus I formulate the concept of a thing: horse, four-footed animal, etc. But really this horse never existed, because each concrete horse has its color. In the way that classical philosophy has operated with the concept since ancient times, as in Democritus, or Aristotle, or Saint Thomas, up to Spinoza, Kant, and Hegel, is *in the void.*

It says: man.

Abstraction does not correspond to reality. It is from the other world, so to speak. It is here that thought finds its most violent internal contradiction.

And it is the basis, to use Hegelian language, of an antithesis which leads us directly to *existence.*

Existentialism is particularly meant to be a philosophy of the concrete. But this is a dream; in concrete reality, one cannot make arguments. Arguments always use concepts, etc. Existentialism is therefore a tragic system of thought because it can never be self-sufficient, it must be simultaneously both an abstract and a concrete philosophy.

Kierkegaard's philosophy is a reaction against Hegel's.

It is beginning with Husserl that existentialism becomes possible, since Husserl's phenomenological method consists of investigations of truth as essence.

It is a description of our consciousness, a sort of application of the Aristotelian method to the self.

But while Aristotle's philosophy is a classification of the world, Husserl's phenomenological method consists of the purification and classification of the phenomena of our consciousness.

Existentialism

Existentialism was born directly from Kierkegaard's attack on Hegel.

In fact, there is not just one existentialist school but several, among others, those of Jaspers, Gabriel Marcel (that sad fool), Sartre . . . But in fact, existentialism is an attitude that comes from Parmenides, Plato, Jesus Christ, Saint Augustine, up to our time.

I shall try to tell you how existential philosophy differs from classical philosophy.

In the first place, as has already been said with respect to Kierkegaard, it is the *opposition between the concrete and the abstract.*

It is an extremely serious and even tragic thing for the mind, as we reason with *concepts,* thus with abstractions.

Tragic because reasoning can be done only through concepts and logic, and general laws cannot be formed without concepts and without logic. On the other hand, *concepts do not exist in reality* (very important).

But there still is an objection which Kierkegaard formulated against Hegel: "Hegelian truth is conceived in advance." The choice of our ideas is not formed as a consequence of an argument, but they are chosen in advance. Reasoning serves only to justify a previous choice. (It is impossible to fight with what the soul has chosen—Zeromski.*)

Hegel conceived his world in advance, in his reason, etc. Therefore, premeditated. Another flaw in abstract reasoning, and it is dramatic for the mind. Because of this, reasoning is not possible.

Under these conditions, how can existentialist reasoning, or a philosophical system like that of Heidegger or Sartre, be possible?

*Stefan Zeromski (1864–1925), Polish novelist and dramatist.

Husserl's phenomenological method came to the aid of the existentialists.

Heidegger was Husserl's favorite pupil. Husserl never forgave Heidegger for having profited from phenomenology for totally different ends, thereby creating the first existentialist system. Why the phenomenological method?

It is a new reduction of the thinking that had already been reduced by Descartes, Feuerbach, and others.

This reduction consists in the following: Husserl says: because we can say nothing about the *noumenon* (thing in itself), we put the *noumenon* in parentheses; that is, that the only thing one can speak of are *the phenomena.*

The *noumenon,* for example, is this chair such as it really is, and the phenomenon is the chair as we see it, or seen by an ant, conditioned by our capacity to see. That concerns not only our physical faculties of perception but also our mental faculties, as Kant showed (namely that time and space derive from us and not from the object in itself).

Husserl says: since we cannot know anything about the *noumenon,* I am putting it in parentheses. About the existence of God, for example, we know nothing.

And, returning to Descartes' famous "cogito ergo sum" (I think, therefore I am), Husserl brackets the *world* and *all the sciences concerning the world* (biology, physics, history). Only the sciences involving our faculties remain, like mathematics, logic, geometry, etc.

He bracketed God and the sciences.

You really see the tremendous repercussions of seeing according to the phenomenological method.

Alas, I do not know whether Isa exists, I have an idea of Isa in my head!* Likewise, I was never born. I was never born in 1904.

I only know that I have the idea of my birth in 1904 in my consciousness, and that I have the idea of 1904, that is to say, of all the past years.

Everything changed in a diabolical way. That changes the universe. There is nothing more than a definitive center which is consciousness and that which passes into consciousness. Consciousness is evidently alone. The possibility of other consciousnesses does not exist.

Life is nothing more than a fact of consciousness. Likewise, logic, history, my future are nothing

---

*Isa Neyman was a friend of Gombrowicz's who sometimes attended his philosophy lectures.

more than facts of my consciousness which I cannot even call "my" consciousness, since "my" consciousness is only a fact of "the" definitive consciousness.

Everything reduces to phenomena in my consciousness. How, in this state of things, can one do philosophy?

For this definitive consciousness, nothing else remains than for it to "judge" itself. As consciousness is conscious of something, so, it is conscious of itself. Consciousness separates itself so to speak into several parts, which can be described as follows: first, second, third consciousness. But this second consciousness can be described by a third consciousness, and this is precisely what I do in speaking of the third consciousness.

Please do not forget that this is an extremely rudimentary manner of presenting phenomenology to you.

There is still one law of consciousness formulated by Husserl, called *"the intentionality" of consciousness,* that is, that consciousness consists in being conscious. But in order to be conscious, one must always be conscious of something. And that means that consciousness can never be empty, separated from the object. This leads directly to Sartre's notion of man, which says that *man is not a being in himself* as objects are, but is a being *"for himself,"* that he is conscious of himself. This leads to a notion of man divided in two, with an empty space. It is for this reason that Sartre's book is called *Nothingness.* This nothingness is a kind of *water spray* or *Niagara Falls* which always goes from the interior to the exterior.

For example, I am conscious of this painting, my consciousness is not only within me, it is in the painting (object of the consciousness). Consciousness is, so to speak, *outside of me.*

When I read that in *Being and Nothingness,* I shouted with enthusiasm, since it is precisely the notion of man which creates form and which cannot really be authentic.

Ferdydurke fortunately appeared in 1937 and *Being and Nothingness* in 1943. And this is why someone kindly credits me with anticipating existentialism. Let us return to our task.

I spoke of Husserl's phenomenological method because it made existential philosophy possible. In truth, existentialism cannot produce any philosophy.

Me, I am alone, concrete, independent of any logic, of any concept.

What to do in this situation?

Be crucified like Jesus Christ?
Be lost in one's pain?
One lives alone, one dies alone.
Impenetrable.

But with the phenomenological method, one can organize the facts of our consciousness concerning our existence. And that is the only thing we are left with.

Husserl's method has been compared to the way to eat an artichoke, that is, that I observe a notion in my consciousness.

Example: the color yellow. I try to reduce it to its purest state, like the artichoke, leaf after leaf. And when we finally reach the heart, we throw ourselves upon it and devour it.

Phenomenology is a descent to the most profound notion, the *last* notion of a phenomenon, and when it is purified, we throw ourselves upon it and swallow it by direct intuition.

I remind you that intuition is direct knowledge without reasoning.

Thus existentialism is the profound and most definitive description of our facts concerning existence.

Sartre appropriated a lot from Heidegger. Heidegger is more creative than Sartre, but Sartre is clearer.

Sartre offered this description of existence. I must speak again of a very profound difference between existentialism and the previous philosophy.

Classical philosophy was rather a philosophy of *things* where even man was treated somewhat like a thing, while existentialism is supposed to be a philosophy of BEING.

Every object is both *object plus being.*

It is true that this difference almost always existed in philosophy, even in Hegel's philosophy of becoming.

But existentialism focused on this and on a single type of BEING, which is precisely existence.

Three different kinds of BEING:

1. The being in itself (being of things).

2. The being for itself (being of dead consciousness. Being independent of that).

3. Living beings or existing beings.

The word "existence" means only conscious human existence, only inasmuch as one is conscious of existence. Men who live in an unconscious manner have no existence.

Animals have no consciousness.

This is practically Sartre's classification. This is precisely the theme of *Being and Nothingness.*

How can one define the characteristics of "the Being in itself," that is, the being of objects?

1. We have to say that only phenomena exist (Husserl). Everything manifests itself as a phenomenon. One cannot say, according to Sartre, that people are intelligent if they express themselves only in stupid deeds. Man is nothing more than what one sees.

Notice that each thing has no limit.

Lamp, etc., are arbitrary definitions sanctified by our language.

One can see that existentialism moves into structuralism.

The Being in itself can be neither created by someone, nor active or passive (since these are human ideas).

The Being in itself is *opaque.*

He is as he is, that is all one can say, he is *immobile.* He is not subject to creation and temporality, and cannot be inferred from something (like created by God).

The Being in itself is a being about which nothing can be asserted, except that it is IN ITSELF such as it is (a little like God).

Curious thing, the *Being for itself,* human existence, is somehow inferior to the Being in itself. It is in itself the *void, nothingness,* formed so to speak in two parts. As if it were cut in two, and it is this which permits it to be conscious of itself.

So it is a secondary being, compared to the Being in itself.

Curious thing: this rudimentary comparison that I have managed to do can seem naïve. Yet it leads to real concepts, for example, that the human being is empty because of the well-known intentionality of consciousness. If a chair is a chair, then consciousness is never identical to itself because one must always be conscious of something. One cannot imagine empty consciousness. The well-known identity principle, A equals A (chair is chair), is not carried out here. The Being of consciousness is, in this sense, an imperfect being. But let us go further.

The Being in itself cannot disappear. It is independent of time and space. It is as it is, nothing more. While *existence, the Being for itself,* is a limited being, with an end, which dies. (This is at least how our existence appears to our consciousness. Existence must be sustained like a flame.)

For Einstein, an object is nothing more than a "curvature of space." A chair stands for an amount of energy, and this energy can transform itself into another object, or remain unchanged energy, while human existence begins and ends (birth and death).

But then, what is man, as *Being for itself* or existence?

1. Man is a thing because he has a body, which is the only way, as body, that he can be in the world. Here Sartre launches into some very subjective reactions: he says that man as body is *excessive*. It provokes nausea, thus the title: *Nausea.*

2. Man is a thing because he is a *fact* (facticity). For example: I have my past, I am already made, defined, achieved. But when I head toward the future, I leave the world of things in order to enter into the fulfillment of myself.

3. Man is a thing by his *situation,* which takes away his freedom.

Here is the well-known question of freedom which makes us responsible for ourselves. Evidently, we have two perfectly contradictory feelings. On the one hand, we are merely the effect of a cause. Example: if I drink, it is because I am thirsty. If, according to Freudianism, I have a complex, it is the result of a shock. On the other hand, we are absolutely sure of being free. No one can take away from me the feeling that it is I myself who decides whether I have to move my hand or not. Indeed, when we contemplate other people, they appear to us as the consequence of a cause.

For a physician, there is no doubt that a patient's illnesses obey causes. This feeling of freedom, which is so strong within us, concerns only ourselves, while we see others as mechanisms. Therefore the *Being in itself* always has its cause as it appears, it has neither beginning nor end. Freedom is uniquely the particularity of the *Being in itself.* There is a rupture here of course between the feelings of universal causality and our feeling of freedom, which is due to the essential difference between scientific knowledge and existential knowledge. This is very important because it defines the limits of science, which can never be the foundation for philosophy, because only consciousness can be conscious of science, whereas science can never be based on consciousness. Moreover, science sees man from the outside, as one object among others.

The difference between the appendix operation from the point of view of the physician, who treats the patient as a mechanism, and the point of view of the patient. For the patient, this operation is *lived.* It is *subjective,* and it must be undergone by him and by no one else. There is another thing: in the past, we felt subject to causality while the future seemed to depend on ourselves. This is why Heidegger said that existential time is the future. Everything that man does may be considered from the point of view of the past. I move my hand because I feel like smoking. Or of the future: I move my hand in order to pick up the pipe.

Therefore we can assert that freedom is a feature only of existence while causality is the feature of the *Being in itself.*

Existentialism is not a science.

In existentialism, the whole is not a mechanism, the sum of the components always means something more than the sum total. Let us imagine that the words which form a sentence are not just a quantity of words but also a meaning. Between the way of seeing man as object, from the outside, characteristic of medicine, of psychology, of history, etc., and that of existentialism, which is to feel, so to speak, *from the inside,* within his being, there is an ABYSS.

Monday, May 5, 1969

Existentialism

Existentialism is subjectivity.

Personally, I am quite subjective and it seems to me that this attitude corresponds to reality.

Subjective man

Concrete man.

Not a concept of man, but Pierre or François, since the concept of man does not exist, says Kierke-gaard.

Because of this, it is monstrously difficult for existentialism to make arguments, since arguments are based on concepts, and only thanks to Heidegger's betrayal which took hold of the phenomenological method, can one speak [*sentence incomplete*].

The existentialist is a *subjective, free* man. He has what one calls free will, unlike a man viewed from the scientific outside, who is always subject to causality, like a mechanism.

This bold theory that man is free seems absolutely mad in a world where everything is cause and effect. It relies on an elementary sensation: we are free and there is no way to convince me that if I move my left hand it is not because I want to. It is not easy to specify what this possibility of freedom is based on.

I imagine that it is based on a difference in time. Time for man is not the past but the future. If one does something, it is not *because of* but rather *in order to.* "I read in order to remind myself," etc.

If in the past, you have causality, in the future, in man's existence, we are dealing with the future.

One can say, more profoundly, that in our consciousness one finds the same internal rupture, which reveals itself, for example, in the physical.

Man, that being *for himself,* is divided in two (with a hole). It is in this nothingness, in this void (the hole), that the concept of *freedom* is introduced. Freedom has an enormous role for Sartre, because it is the foundation of his moral system.

Sartre is a moralist, and it is curious that the same deviation observed by Husserl in Descartes is produced again in French philosophy.

Descartes, in an extremely categorical way, reduces thought to a single description of consciousness, but suddenly, *frightened* by the annihilation of God, of the world, he betrays himself. He recognized God's existence. This already deduces, from the existence of God, the existence of the world.

Now, in Sartre, in my view, we are dealing with the same cowardice. There are perhaps fifteen pages in *Being and Nothingness* where Sartre makes some dramatic efforts to logically justify a phenomenon which seems absolutely evident, the existence of a man other than "self." For example, the phenomenon of Witold's existence is the same as that of a chair.

Sartre analyzes all the systems: Kant, Hegel, Husserl, and he demonstrates that none of them has any possibility of recognizing the other man. Why? Because to be man is to be subject. It is to have a consciousness which recognizes everything else as object. If I admitted that Witold too has a consciousness, then inevitably I myself am an object for Witold, who is the subject. It is impossible to be subject and object at the same time. Here Sartre was frightened. His highly developed ethics refuses to admit that there is no other man because there are no longer any moral obligations. The other being object.

Sartre, who was always torn between Marxism (scientific) and existentialism (the opposite), was frightened just like Descartes. He stated quite simply and honestly that even though it was impossible to recognize the existence of others, there is no other way than to recognize it as an obvious fact. There all of Sartre's philosophy, all its creative potential, dramatically collapses, and this man, gifted with extraordinary genius, becomes a sad fellow (Marxism-existentialism) who, essentially, is obliged to produce a philosophy of concessions. His thinking became a compromise between Marxism and existentialism. And so all his books became the basis of a moral system in which everything already serves to support a preconceived theory. Now the basis of this moral system is the well-known *Sartrean freedom.*

He says, "I am free, I feel free. Therefore I always have the possibility to choose. This choice is limited because man is always in a situation, and he can choose only within that situation. Example: I can stay on the bed or I can walk, but I cannot choose to fly because I do not have wings. There is free choice for which man is responsible. If I refuse to choose between two possibilities, this is also a way of choosing a third position. If one does not want to choose between communism and anti-communism, there is neutrality." Sartre also says that man is the creator of values. This is the direct consequence of a stubborn atheism, the most consistent in all of philosophy.

Such is the situation: since we have lost the notion of God, so we ourselves become *creators of values,* because of our absolute freedom. And, in this sense, we can do what we want. Example: I can, if it is my choice, find it a good idea to assassinate X or not to assassinate him. The two possibilities exist, but in choosing them, I choose myself as assassin, or not.

Here I believe I recognize an excess of intellectualism and decadence (the weakening) of sensitivity in philosophy. Philosophers, except Schopenhauer, seem to be people comfortably seated in their easy chairs who treat pain with absolutely Olympian disdain, which will vanish the day they go to the dentist and cry *ouch, ouch, Doctor.* Sartre, in his theoretical disdain for pain, states that for a man who chooses pain as good, torture can become a celestial pleasure. This assertion seems very doubtful to me and characteristic of the French bourgeoisie, which, very fortunately, was spared for a long time from great pain. Despite Sartre's assertion that freedom is limited by the situation and what is called "facticity" (the fact, for example, that we have a body, that we are a fact, a phenomenon, in the world), despite all his limitations, he goes too far.

Existential man is

concrete,

alone,

made of nothingness,

thus free.

He is condemned to freedom and he can *choose* himself.

What happens if we choose, for example, frivolity and not authenticity, falseness and not truth? As there is no hell, there is no punishment. From the existential point of view, the only punishment is that this man has no true existence. Therefore he is not an extant thing. Here is a play on words, as much from Heidegger as from Sartre, which the one who chose the supposed non-existence will really make fun of.

What is the future of existentialism?

Very great.

I do not agree with the superficial judgments for which existentialism is a trend. Existentialism is a consequence of a basic fact of the internal rupture of consciousness which is manifested not only in man's inherent qualities, but—extremely curious fact—is evident in physics for example, where you have two ways of perceiving reality:

—corpuscular

—undulatory

Example: theories of light.

Now, both theories are right, as experience demonstrates, but they are contradictory. You have the same phenomenon in the physics concept concerning electrons, where there are two different ways of seeing them, both of which are correct and contradictory. Now, in my view, man is divided between the subjective and the objective, irreparably and for all time. This is a kind of wound we have which is impossible to heal, and of which we are more and more conscious. In a number of years, it will be even "bloodier," since it can only grow with the evolution of consciousness.

The profound truth of Hegel's dialectics (thesis-synthesis) appears here. It is impossible, under these conditions, to ask that a man be harmonious, that he be able to resolve anything. Fundamental impotence.

No solution at all.

In the light of these thoughts, literature which considers that we can organize the world is the most idiotic thing imaginable.

A sad writer who thinks himself master of reality is a ridiculous thing. Hah! Hah! Hah! Phew!

Tuesday, May 6, 1969

Freedom in Sartre

Freedom is an experience.

It is linked to future time, which is the time of human existence.

It is marked by finality, which is the opposite of *causality.* In the world of *causality,* one does something because one is obliged by a cause to do so. In the world of finality, one does something for something. I pick up the pipe in order to smoke. Freedom is always achieved in a *situation,* that is, that in each situation I have a freedom of choice, but I cannot choose something which is outside of the situation. For example, I can walk or sit, but I cannot fly.

Finally, it is freedom which is the foundation of all value. We must not forget that atheism is at the root of all Sartrean existentialism. He said that it is not as easy to follow atheism through to the end as he did. When one is there, at the limit, one sees that, since God does not exist, all qualities are established by me, by my freedom. I can, for example, establish torture as the supreme good: the moral and the immoral are two things which are decided in complete freedom. But as in all of Sartre's work, we immediately notice a retreat. One would think that he is the most absolute immoralist, but no. He is 100 percent moralist. If I understand this aspect of Sartrean philosophy correctly, it is rather artificial.

1. Man in his freedom chooses himself by choosing his *values* (replace quality by value). This depends on his free choice. But on my choice depends what Heidegger called authentic existence and consequently, real life or a different world.

2. Consequently, man is responsible for his self, but man is responsible also for the world, since *to choose oneself* means to choose the world. Therefore I can choose myself as Hitlerite, Nazi, and choose a Nazi world.

Sartre was asked: why cannot we choose Hitlerism if we are the free creator of our values, and what obliges me, for example to choose Marxism?

This rather elementary contradiction was not, according to my humble opinion, sufficiently clarified by Sartre, because evidently morality is a limitation of freedom, even if reasons are needed for choosing that limitation.

Here on the subject of freedom, Sartre is very categorical. He says that the choice depends only on us, there are no pre-established values, it is our choice which creates them. One could imagine that man, with all his freedom, is nevertheless condemned to satisfy the fundamental necessities of life, such as eating. But this also depends on me. If I choose suicide, food loses all value for me. And from this absolute responsibility of man to himself is born the characteristic anguish of existentialism, as much for Heidegger as for Kierkegaard and Sartre.

This anguish is the anguish of nothingness. When I am afraid, says Heidegger, I am afraid of something, such as a tiger. But if I do not fear anything specific, that is anguish. This anguish is born, according to Sartre, from our responsibility regarding our existence. One could ask, for instance, how can I be absolutely free to choose myself, if, born short, I want to be tall? Now the choice is not the choice of a fact, it is the choice of a value. I cannot freely choose my height, but that depends on my considering smallness as a quality or a defect.

There are still other impossibilities for our freedom, deriving from what one calls man's *facticity.* We must not forget that man by his body, by his mechanism, belongs to the world dictated by causality, since if we are stabbed, evidently we are going to bleed, like every other animal. Freedom manifests itself only in existence, in that specific being which is the Being for itself.

Anguish is anguish before myself, such that I am not yet, since I must choose myself. It comes from the consciousness of freedom and it is the fundamental structure of man. Most people do not feel it, because they flee from these problems and in fleeing it they affirm it.

Sartre defines this as an act of *bad faith,* which is, according to him, an act by which we want to deceive (distort) ourselves, to lie to ourselves, and these people reject will, but this act of rejection is also free, and they know it. From there, the reassuring myth which lets us forget our terrible solitude, and our responsibility to ourselves. Sartre calls that man who hides from this responsibility a "bastard."

There is a famous short story by Sartre, *L'Enfance d'un chef,* in which a young man, panicked in the face of his homosexual tendencies, in order not to choose to be homosexual, chooses to be anti-Semitic, and he becomes anti-Semitic for everyone. This is his characteristic, his duty, etc. In fleeing from our fundamental responsibility, we choose to be another character, or we choose absolute values such as God, the laws of nature, etc. So now, Sartre defines what his own morality consists of.

It is choosing freedom and affirming freedom.

This is the basis of Sartre's communism. One could wonder why Sartre, in choosing communism, a system defined by values, is not a bastard. It is that every other social system signifies the exploitation of man by man, thus a limitation on freedom. In choosing communism, we choose freedom.

Wednesday, May 7, 1969

The View of Others

We are subject to other people's point of view. Naturally it is necessary to recognize the existence of others. It is an *obvious fact*. Sartre does not find any philosophical reasons to justify it. This view of others takes away our freedom, defines us. For the other, we are a thing, an object, we have a character, etc. This view of others is contrary to our freedom, but it is only in recognizing the other's freedom that I free myself from his gaze. All of Sartrean morality consists *of recognizing and of affirming freedom.*

Consequently, Sartre naturally insists that every writer be engaged, that he belong to the left, and that he be subject to its rigorous rules! In other, less successful works, Sartre tries above all (in *The Critique of Dialectical Reason*) to reconcile existentialism with Marxism, which naturally is nonsense.

Sunday, May 11, 1969

Heidegger

Before Sartre there was Martin Heidegger, who is undoubtedly more creative. Born in 1889, professor at Freiburg, and author of the book *Being and Time,* 1927.

It should be said right away that Heidegger was supposed to write a second volume, but he ultimately never managed to organize his thinking. His thinking is difficult and tortured.

Existentialism quite simply means to describe the rapport of our consciousness with our existence, in other words, what are for man the most profound, the most definitive aspects of existence. We proceed by the elimination of the more superficial lateral aspects, and we reach the deeper, more authentic concepts regarding our existence. This phenomenological method is not concerned with God, etc., but only with what is in our consciousness, when it confronts our specific being, our existence. It is phenomenological ontology.

Ontology means the science of Being (existence). Phenomenological means that there are only phenomena, and one must not look for something behind the phenomena. In this sense, this method is completely atheistic.

Heidegger said that complex arguments are not needed as much as heroic naïveté.

General ontology is the main problem: what is Being? Here we rediscover a drop of Schopenhauerism: by the analysis of our existence, of what "Being" means for us, we can reach that general problem which was supposed to be resolved in the second volume of *Being and Time.*

First question:

> What is Being?
>
> What is existence?
>
> (What is a form of "Being").

Second question: What is the meaning of this existence?

Heidegger says that everyone knows, but no one can answer. It is Saint Augustine who said about time: "I know what it is when they don't ask me, but when they ask me, I don't know."

Classical philosophy wanted to explain Being in a rational way and not by experimenting. We begin, says Heidegger, by man's Being, and afterward we move to being in general.

Now, first, we must notice that only man is capable of questioning himself on the subject of his existence. But how?

This is not an introspection, because introspection and psychoanalysis regenerate through contact with the phenomena of existence but not with existence itself.

What is existence, that is, man's specific being? He says:

It defines itself by what he calls "*Da-sein*," "to be there" (over there). To be man. To exist as a man. The "*Seindes*" is a way for things to exist, an absurd atemporal way (a chair, it is but does not know it).

But man is also a "*Seindes*," and he is conscious of that: being a thing. But he also transcends this (transcendent: that which within me navigates toward the exterior), since man is a thing but he is also something more. He extends beyond the thing. He is transcendent. The word "*Sein*," to be.

Existentialism (Heidegger)

The confrontation of our consciousness with our existence.

It is not about man, but about the human being and the way of being, so to speak, human.

"*Seindes*" is the way of being things, senseless, absurd.

You clearly see how existentialism does not talk about the lack of meaning of an idea, or of the meaning of God, but of the way that things have of being. Things are absurd because they are here without doing anything so to speak. They are as they are. They have no history. They are not in time. It's true that a thing can deteriorate in time, but it undergoes this passively, it is always that way. The "*Sein,*" to be meaningful, significant. Now, the "*Da-sein*" gives meaning to the being of things.

In this first place, it is an affirmation of man. Next, it is about giving a meaning to things, that is, *to men.*

We already said that things do not have limits. We cannot say where a table ends and where the floor begins, because in truth, it is always about matter composed of atoms. Energy for Einstein is nothing more than a "curvature" in space, and the thing is a definite thing because man defines it. Man does this in view of his necessities and his plans. The chair is for sitting, the table is for writing. Therefore, the "*Da-sein,*" the higher being, existence, forms a higher being which rightly is a significant being, a human being, an existence. Heidegger says that absurd existence is "ontic," while meaningful, higher existence leads to ontology.

There again is something important which inspired Sartre (who appropriated a lot from Heidegger).

Heidegger says that man's essence is his existence, that man is not a definite thing. There are no models of man—as for example in Catholic philosophy—but man is an existence in the process of making itself. Subtle but profound difference. One cannot say that someone is man; one can say only that he becomes man, that he achieves himself as human existence. It is because of this that Sartre ascribes to man a total freedom to choose himself.

Heidegger differentiates the existence that he calls banal and the existence that he calls authentic. Therefore man exists on two levels:

1. daily existence, *banal*

2. and *authentic* existence.

Kierkegaard made the same classification, but he added religious life. Now, for Heidegger, as for Sartre or Marx, religion is an invention of men to avoid confrontation with the true human condition. And daily life is not necessarily and entirely banal.

Man can exist in the two dimensions of the banal and the authentic.

So, one will ask, what is the importance and value of this authentic existence.

Man, says Heidegger, must create himself. As he is not a thing, well then! he must become "man." Banal life simply means to flee from oneself. This is in order to forget and to lose oneself. To become man is only one possibility. One does not use the word "I," but one uses "one." "One" goes to the movies. "One" has political opinions. And man identifies himself with his social function. "One" is an engineer, etc. You understand in which direction Heidegger's probing is going. Man *must truly become man.*

In light of this idea, you see that there are very few people who have human lives. Our relationship with things is overall a utilitarian relationship, dominated by what one calls "*Sorge*" in German.

Sein und Zeit (Being and Time) starts by establishing man's constant preoccupation with the preservation of life, the "*Sorge.*"

In the psychological sense, curiosity is the superficial connection of man. What are they talking about? In the more profound sense, it is an interpretation of man, of the world, of being, of scientific, philosophical, or religious problems.

It is also a way to make existence commonplace, to flee from existence, a way of replacing the profound sense of life by a superficial and limited science. The dramatic thing about man (and here again, Sartre comes to mind) is that man gives a meaning to things by his existence. Now, in dealing with science, for example, he gives it an inauthentic meaning.

He falsifies. *Existentialism refrains from science.* Moving from this inauthentic sphere to the authentic does not consist of a process of culture, of knowledge, but of what he calls a *leap,* a decision to accept anguish and its revelation. Anguish has a terrible role in existentialism.

How can anguish be defined?

Fear is the fear of something.

Anguish is the fear of nothing,

of non-meaning,

of not giving some meaning to the world,

and of losing oneself.

It is an experience of nothingness and one of the main sources of the mania for nothingness which has stupidly taken hold of European culture and literature.

For me, the stupidity comes from an extremism which is in no way man's true reality. Man is a being who needs a moderate temperature; neither the microcosmos nor the macrocosmos is man's domain. Modern physics proves that some perfectly correct laws for the micro and macro world are not carried out in our human reality.

For man, a straight line will always be the shortest distance between two points and not the curve, as demonstrated by astronomical dimensions. I am of the school of Montaigne, and I favor a more moderate attitude: we must not succumb to theories, but must know that *systems have a very short life and not allow ourselves to be imposed on.*

As you see, it is a magnificent theme for literature!

Existence is made of nothingness (Hegelian idea), and can only be discovered by the existence of nothingness. (Example: the duel scene in Dostoyevsky's *The Possessed*). Man must not be fooled by his form. Go further and say that man escapes from all definition, from all theory, from whatever you want.

Man's relationship with his most profound thinking is characterized by his immaturity. It is like a schoolboy who strives to say important things with a frivolous aim of *surpassing* others, in order to be more scholarly than others.

We must live and let live.

Unpremeditated literature.

High spirituality is a rare thing, and the human race is distinguished by its differences. *Each man has his world.*

In general, nothingness was considered by all of philosophy to be a dialectical contradiction of being, first you think that something is, and only afterward can you get to the idea of nothingness in saying that in removing something, there is emptiness.

Now, Heidegger gave a famous lecture on why *Being exists rather than nothing?*

For Heidegger, it is the Being which appears secondarily as a contradiction of nothingness.

1. nothingness
2. Being.

This definition can seem rather unfounded, but actually it leads to an extremely curious and true experience: human existence is in constant opposition to nothingness. Man always threatened by death and annihilation persists like a flame which wants to be revived, fed.

To conclude, a general characteristic of existence, according to Heidegger.

1. It is "*Sorge,*" concern.

Human life is by no means assured, but endlessly wants conquests, life is to conquer what one does not have.

2. Human beings are limited and have an end precisely because they have nothingness within them. Authentic existence asserts man's finiteness. It has moral constants. It does not permit having a clear conscience. Never are we what we want to be, but we still want to be. Man is essentially unhappy because he is limited. We should add some very important things about time.

It is Heidegger who introduced the notion of "completed future." Man's time is always the future. He is never there where he is. He is always transcendent. Time for Heidegger is complicated. He gets confused. The essentials of this philosophy have been explained.

Death does not exist. When death comes, one does not know that one is dying.

Man is for death.

The problem of death preoccupies human thought, without arriving at a result.

How to explain what I am?

And what I no longer am? not?

We know nothing.

When I die, the world no longer exists.

The merit of structuralism is that it seriously deals with language, since we are (since philosophy is) a verbalism without end.

Marx 1818–1883

Marx knew Hegel in his youth, but at age nineteen, he indicated in a letter to his father that Hegel did not satisfy him.

And why?

It was the abstract element, the abstract logic, which distanced Marx from Hegel.

It is true that he appropriated a lot from Hegel, but he revolutionized the very meaning of philosophy.

He said that the problem of philosophy is not to understand the world but to change it.

Man is in relation to the external world. He needs to dominate nature, and there lies his real problem, all the rest is *frippery.*

Marx said that philosophy must not be aristocratic, that is, done by men outside of communal life, but must be done on the scale of the average man, of the man who has needs and lives in society.

One can, Marx said, conduct a revision of thinking and values from top to bottom. What comes from on top is inevitably a luxury, an ornament. But what comes from below is reality. One must therefore go from a lower to a higher consciousness.

From Hegel, he took the idea of becoming in a dialectical process (thesis, antithesis, synthesis).

According to Hegel: the idea of history which is achieved precisely by antinomies and which is proper to man, as I remind you that for Hegel, nature is always the same, it repeats itself. The planets always run in the same way, and the evolution of the lower species, insects, animals, is extremely slow and invisible.

How does the world appear, according to Marx?

The first aspect is its *materialism.* Marxism is the negation of religion. He considered religion as a product of men to run from danger. And this is an instrument of the higher class to dominate the lower class.

Materialism constitutes the negation of idealism, of all metaphysics, of all recourse to ideas. For Marxism, there is only the *brutal, concrete reality of life.*

Second aspect: Marxism defines itself by the well-known formula, *consciousness depends on being.*

For a classical philosopher, consciousness was a primary, elementary thing. Everything was for consciousness, and nothing could determine it.

Marx proceeds to a new reduction of human reason. It is a sociological reduction of thought.

The reductions in succession being:

1. [*word missing*] reduction

2. anthropological reduction

3. phenomenological reduction (Husserl)

4. sociological reduction (Marx)

5. Nietzsche, who reduces philosophy to life.

In order to understand the evolution of thinking, one must know these reductions.

Sociological reduction means that consciousness is determined by existence. This means making consciousness an instrument of life, which gradually developed, beginning with the lowest species by a process of adaptation, of dialectical development, finally by a natural process as with everything.

This means that consciousness is a function of our necessities, of our relationship with nature. But since man does not depend only on nature but also and above all on society, on historic conditions produced by that society, consciousness is formed by that society. Consciousness is therefore above all a function of human history.

The third aspect: need creates value. If you are, for example, in the Sahara Desert, a glass of water can signify an enormous thing for you, while if you are in Vence with the water of the Foux, then it loses its value.

This thesis seems absolutely correct to me. Observe that, for example, it is at the basis of my critique of painting and contrary also to all forms of anarchy, all nihilism, and finally, to arbitrary, existentialist theories, according to which it is not the cause incarnated in a necessity which creates value, but the goals that man proposes in complete freedom.

For example, according to Sartre, a man needs water in the desert because he chooses life and not death. For Marxism, a living being is obliged to choose life and one cannot speak here of free choice.

HISTORY according to the Marxist interpretation.

The history of humanity comes from the necessity to technically dominate nature.

Now, the growing consciousness of humanity lets him organize a society and a state which are above all a system for the production of goods.

In this organization, one man must be subject to another, such that it is through the exploitation of one man by another that one arrives at the accumulation of goods. The man who forms a group is subject to the laws of the group, which wants to be strong, and this strength is the consequence of the exploitation of man by man. For example, the army which obeys a single man through generals, etc., or slaves or finally castes, different stages of the feudal systems, classes.

It is man who obliges man to work.

We thus reach the basic notion, so dear to Marxists.

This basis is the mass of the exploited. The dominant class forms the superstructure which creates philosophy, religion, law, which in a word, *organizes consciousness.* All of this actually serves secretly to maintain the exploitation.

Religion, for example, establishes that author-
ity comes from God and the unfortunate of this
world will find Paradise. The profound and unique
meaning of religion is quite simply to transfer justice to another world.

Christianity, which began as a revolution of
slaves in Rome, nevertheless had a metaphysical com-
ponent: God. But through the church He became
an instrument of exploitation.

When we look at prevailing morality, we see
that it is mainly concerned with maintaining the
right of ownership and imposing bourgeois morality on the proletariat.

The essence of philosophy resides in a con-
templative attitude. It does not want to change the
world. It escapes into metaphysics. In short, it is reason separated from its foundation, a superstructure
which seeks to hide its dependency. It seeks absolute
values and it is not concerned with necessities. Our
law is a system which seeks to consolidate the right
of ownership and exploitation. You see here that
Marxism reveals myth, just like Freudianism or
Nietzsche. It consists in showing that behind our so-
called "noble" feelings hide complexes, cowardice,
and finally, the filth of life. One of the great merits

of Nietzsche, who effectuated an extremely perspicacious critique of pure attitudes, is to have shown that our mind is made of the same material as everything else.

All this leads us to discover, so to speak, man's first nature. The second is a nature deformed by men, by the necessities of this system of exploitation that they call society, whose purpose is to produce goods by using other men. We are in an economic system which deforms our consciousness.

You have seen how religion, morality, philosophy, law are made in order to mystify and to keep the slave in his bondage.

Here we move on to the well-known theory of *surplus value.*

Capitalists, that is to say, members of the upper class, buy labor as if it were merchandise, thus at the best possible price. This better price represents the bare minimum that the worker needs to eat and to father children.

Surplus value is formed this way because the worker produces much more than what he is paid; the rest goes to capitalism.

The worker always produces more than what he is paid.

Such is *surplus value*. The worker's labor is subject, like all merchandise, to Adam Smith's famous economic law, according to which if supply is greater than demand, the value of the merchandise decreases.

It is this law which explains the process of devaluation. To curb devaluation, supply, that is, production, must be increased.

If the currency is devalued, we need more francs each time. As the surplus value goes into the capitalist's pocket, then the workers, being poor, must offer their labor each time at lower prices. This is how the devaluation of labor and the increase of capital are produced, an anonymous force, outside the human element: that which produces the famous *alienation*.

Alienated man, that is, he who cannot be himself, is obliged to serve as a machine instead of having his normal life.

This theory is fine, but in my view, it does not apply to capitalism.

Capital is used to create other wealth, but this exploitation of man by man is not done so much for the happiness of the individual. Capitalism is not exclusively beneficial to the capitalist, since if the capitalist is able to consume his money, he cannot buy more than one hundred hats or a yacht, etc., each year. Where does the rest of his money go? To other factories, other industries, etc., and this is the way that humanity's technical power becomes greater each time. This exploitation of man by man is a fundamental necessity for human progress, which is extremely difficult for the individual.

And now we move on to the "sweets," that is, to

Revolution

Capitalism has this particularity: large capital consumes the smaller, and is concentrated in a very small group of men. Marx anticipated that because of this evolution of capital, on the one hand a small group of multimillionaires would form, and on the other, an enormous crowd of proletarians which [*sentence incomplete*].

And this is how the proletarian revolution is going to happen, which is an inevitable necessity.

Where in this regard is Marxism in 1969?

The big crisis in Marxism stems quite simply from the fact that—as shown by the situation in the

East—one works badly and produces very little. And why? Life is hard; if you do not force men to work, naturally they will not work.

The paradox requires, and it is such an obvious paradox, all the bad faith of a certain left-wing faction not to recognize it: the only country in the world which has more or less liquidated the proletariat, except among the Blacks, is the glorious United States, that is, the capitalists. The Socialists, on the other hand, are going bankrupt everywhere for the simple reason that no one is interested either to produce, nor to force others to do so, because there is no interest at stake.

Today the only hope for communists is for communism to work better in highly developed countries, which is sheer nonsense, since I only need to talk to my masseur five minutes to see that this is absolutely impossible, since man becomes even more egoistical in a rich society than in a poor society.

The Chinese. This is pure Stalinism! Each Chinese person, in news reports on China, shouts like a soldier. It is a terror.

Chinese production evidently increased, but it has not at all increased as one would believe! These last years were a great disillusionment.

Marxism gives hope to the dispossessed.

Marxist thought has served overall to unmask [*sentence incomplete*], but all philosophical thought is generally utopian and leads nowhere.

For me, the Marxist question was absolutely badly put because they asked it from the moral point of view of "justice." But the real problem is not moral, it is economic. To increase wealth is the priority, the distribution of wealth is a secondary thing.

They ask the question from the moral point of view because it is easier, naturally, and permits making lovely sentences.

We see, for example, that in the West the capitalist system succeeded in increasing production enormously, thanks above all to technology, so that the standard of living increased for everyone, whereas they get nowhere with the loveliest sentences. Production drops. Everything stays at the same level, everything slacks off in bureaucracy and anonymity.

There is an elementary thing: if you allow men to deploy all their energy and their intelligence, inevitably one will dominate the other, one will be superior to the other. But in this case, you obtain a huge amount of energy, whereas if you want equality between men, then naturally you must curb this possibility of superiority.

The future of Marxism?

I imagine that in twenty or thirty years, they will discard Marxism.

If the upper class remains as stupid and blind as it is now, and if it relinquishes power to the masses, then we must prepare for a period of regression which will last until the production of a new, strong upper class. But if the right stands firm and does not allow that "guilty conscience," which is actually typical of Marxists, to be imposed on it, then the matter can be resolved by huge galloping advancements in technology, which, according to my rough calculations, can radically change the world in twenty or thirty years. We shall have little wings to fly . . .

Fascism is a revolution backwards.

The big defect in the upper class is that it is essentially a class of consumption. Consequently, it is accustomed to conveniences, becomes lazy, delicate, and degenerate. But now the upper class is increasingly composed of engineers, producers, scientists, intellectuals, lastly, some working people.

I notice a misuse of language by the left which made fascism a terrifying thing. So, the word "worker" does not mean a physician who works hard from morning to night, but rather it means a street sweeper who works for five minutes and then looks at the wall, etc. You see that even language has been falsified.

Leftists are imperialists. They do not understand that they are aristocrats and the first thing that a revolution will do will be to liquidate them, as they did in Poland.

According to Marxism, we are faced with a distorted humanity. It is exploitation which is the source of power. It is our consciousness which is distorted, because it adapted to a system of exploitation it does not want to admit to.

Marxism is an attempt at demystification.

In a philosophical sense, Marxism does not posit an exact idea of the world, but only a liberation of consciousness so that it may react in an authentic and not deformed way to the world and man.

Realization of Marxism

1. Marx's thesis is that Marxism is an absolute historical necessity which occurs due to inexorable economic laws, by the concentration of capital in a little group that will be annihilated by the huge mass of the destitute. Marxists want to introduce the dictatorship of the proletariat, not democracy but dictatorship.

What they call "popular democracy" is a camouflage. This dictatorship of the proletariat must definitively destroy the bourgeoisie and nationalize the means of production (mines, farmland, factories, industries, all forms of exploitation of the worker by the employer).

In this first phase, that of dictatorship, it is the State which must dominate everything, to limit individual freedom and to introduce revolution into the world. In this first phase, each person will be paid according to his services.

2. The second phase is the "celestial" phase of Marxism.

It is a question of the gradual liquidation of the State. When human nature is changed, when we arrive at the standardization of consciousness, then, instead of a State, we shall have small "cooperative" organisms in which each person will freely adapt to a universal order based on justice: this is the DREAM of noble souls! In this idiotic phase, each person will be paid not according to his merits or services but according to his necessities. This is the postulate of justice, since every man has the right to live.

Marxism

This "radiant" phase will occur in a distant future, in an indeterminate time.

Here is where the dialectic of Hegelian history enters, which is gradually going to achieve this transformation, as Marxism has quite a strong notion of imperfection. It knows that things can evolve only slowly and must pass through intermediary phases far from perfection.

In this Marxist thought, the proletariat is a kind of saint, as well as being an elementary force.

1. The proletariat has nothing to lose nor to keep. Everything to destroy.

2. It has only necessities. It is not corrupted by values.

3. It is a class with a universal character, at the very root of all social structure.

4. It is a victim of economic production.

The liberation of the proletariat by revolution is a fundamental condition of all social order. And it is the liberation of need as a source of values.

A second time. We see here that Marxism is not an ideology or a truth, it is just simply the freedom from human needs as a source of values.

The revolution, therefore, is going to free *all* men from natural needs, and on the basis of this freedom, the values will be created by themselves. It must be clearly understood that Marxism is not a revolution of ideas but rather a revolution between concrete men. It is a liberation of man.

The new ideas: future thought is unpredictable and will be created by itself in this new human order.

The politics: organization of action in order to reach a goal.

Praxis is conscious, practical action. According

to Marx, thought must materialize in action. The idea must change itself into an historical force.

Contemplation goes to hell.

Marxism declares the impossibility of all non-materialized theory.

Nietzsche

Nietzsche, like Kant and Schopenhauer, was Polish!*

1844–1900

Nietzsche: the nerves of Shelley, the stomach of Carlyle, and the soul of a young lady.

Nietzsche's immediate genealogy:

Darwin (theory of evolution by struggle)

---

*Kant's hometown, Königsberg (today, Kaliningrad, Russia), was claimed by the Poles, who called it Królewiec. Schopenhauer was from Danzig, which was also claimed by the Poles under the name of Gdánsk. Nietzsche, as well, even though born in Röcken in Prussian Saxony, was deluded by the idea, apparently unfounded, that his ancestors were Polish noblemen ("I am a pure-blooded Polish gentleman," *Ecce Homo*, 1888).

Spencer (English philosopher, theory of evolution from simple to compound, multiple)

Bismarck

Schopenhauer.

Nietzsche was not a philosopher in the strict sense: he wrote aphorisms, some notes.

In order to understand Nietzsche, it is necessary to understand an idea as simple as that of raising cows.

A cattleman is going to try to improve the species in such a way that he will let the weakest cows die and will keep the strongest cows and bulls for breeding.

All of Nietzschean morality finds its basis here.

The human race is like all the others; it is improved by a struggle and a natural selection done by life itself.

Here we see the most sensational and the most provocative aspect of this philosophy: it is the opposition to Christianity, which, according to Nietzsche, was a morality of the weak imposed on the strong, harmful to the human race and, therefore, immoral.

Of course, this attitude was revolutionary and turned all the value systems upside down.

Nietzsche—and this is his major distinction from Schopenhauer—*is on the side of* LIFE.

I point out to you that human thinking, beginning with Kant, increasingly looks for life, evolution, or existence. There is a deep concern of the mind which begins to distrust abstract systems and feels life itself is increasingly threatened.

Now, Nietzsche, already in his first work on the source of Greek tragedy, set Dionysus (god of wine, of orgies, and of vital ecstasy) against Apollo (god of tranquillity, of esthetics, and of contemplation). In Greek tragedy, it is the chorus who represented Dionysus, while Apollo expressed himself through dialogue.

Dionysus is the strength of the human race, of life, while Apollo is the individual, weak and mortal.

This opposition between Apollo and Dionysus still appears today. Example: Beethoven. Nietzsche considers pessimism to be a weakness, condemned by life and optimism, a superficial (Canadian!) thing.*

What remains?

A leap into the depths: it is tragic optimism which remains for man, adoration of life and of its cruel laws, despite all the weakness of the individual.

*Gombrowicz's wife, Rita, is Canadian.

In Greece, it is Socrates, Plato, and Aristotle who represent the equilibrium condemned by Nietzsche, while Euripides and Aristophanes proclaim vital law.

Here it is necessary to provide a secondary clarification: why is Greece so important for us? Because in Greece, for the first time, rational man comes to fruition, man formed by Reason. So that is why Greek philosophy and art become so important for us, because all of Europe and modern humanity come from Greece.

Nietzsche's strength consisted of an extremely perspicacious and cruel critique of all our ideas, of the human soul, of morality and of philosophy. He demonstrated that philosophical thought does not come to fruition outside of life, as if philosophers looked at the world and its evolution from a distance, but this thought is bathed in life and always expresses life when it is not falsified.

Nietzsche was a great forerunner in this sense, although he appropriated much from Schopenhauer, especially that which concerns freedom of instinct, even if in a completely opposite sense.

For Nietzsche, life is not good, but we are condemned to life. This leads to paradoxes, such as his admiration for cruelty, harshness (without mercy), and for the whip, weapons. A "military" philosophy.

In Nietzsche, we find three dominant concepts.

In *Zarathustra* (of which he sold only forty copies and gave seven of them as gifts):

1. God is dead. This means that humanity has reached its maturity. Faith in God is already anachronistic. Man ends up all alone in the cosmos. Nothing but life.

2. (Stupid idea.) The ideal of the superman. Man is a transient phenomenon that must be overtaken. Man is thus problematic. He is a bridge and not an end in himself.

His notion of man: we are nothing more than a means to reach a higher being. Now, love and devotion for this future man, the superman, are more important than love of others.

3. The Eternal Return.

This is originally an idea of scientific origin, born on the one hand from the notion of infinite time, and on the other, from the idea of causality.

Entropy. Loss of energy through radiation.

Nietzsche starts from an original cause which produces all the other causes, cause-effects, etc.

Automatic process from cause to effect, thanks to which we arrive at the present moment.

This will be exceeded by other cause-effects and finally will vanish, and again the first cause will return, etc., and we shall arrive again at the same situation.

As time is infinite, this will repeat itself eternally.

This is a naïve and outmoded idea, because the idea of causality works only in the phenomenological world; it can be useful for science and can be verified through experimentation, but it is limited by our means of perception.

We cannot therefore speak of the thing in itself, of God, of eternity.

Nietzsche starts from a scientific idea of causality and constructs a metaphysical system of life.

He was seduced by the supreme affirmation of life.

Without God, there are no external laws.

—The only law for Nietzsche is the affirmation of life.

—It is an anti-Christian and atheistic philosophy.

—It is not so easy to be an atheist.

Sunday, May 25

In giving the general characteristics of existentialism, I forgot a very important thing.

For classical philosophy, the philosopher was an observer who looked at life, but he was outside of life.

Kierkegaard already attacked this attitude in saying that the philosopher is in life.

Philosophy is an act of existence. It is too easy to consider the philosopher as a privileged being.

In each philosophy, there is a fundamental choice which is arbitrary, and everything else, system, reasoning, only serve to justify this choice—to prove that it responds to reality. This *idea of the fundamental choice*, arbitrary, was taken up again by Sartre: it is an act of freedom by our faculty for creating values.

And this fundamental choice in Sartre can go as far as the choice of negation as value: if I choose death and not life, everything that leads me to death, for example, the lack of food—becomes a positive value. Moreover, it is for this reason that Sartre was so interested in Genet, because Genet chose evil; naturally this is a foolish thing, because every police chief knows quite well that Genet did not choose anything. He started with some petty thefts, etc., and so he became a thief by an imperceptible mechanism, minute by minute. This fundamental choice establishes what they call *existential psychoanalysis.*

I return to this important point about existentialism: *the philosopher is in life,* one of the major currents of our thinking during the 19th century.

The path of this Western thought could be defined by the great questions it asked.

1. The reduction of thought. Thought for Kant becomes conscious of its limits. It already knows that one cannot demonstrate, for example, the existence of God, but that it is just as impossible to demonstrate that God does not exist.

Through the consecutive reductions of Feuerbach, of Marx (consciousness as a function of life, "being defines consciousness"), the phenomenological reduction of Husserl, where already philosophy does not seek the reality of things nor the truth, but only a kind of putting in order of the facts of our consciousness, and finally the psychoanalytical reduction of Freud which, in my view, does not have much to do with these reductions, since it is of a scientific nature.

Reduction is the dominant characteristic of the 19th century.

2. The other problem is more difficult, that of life, of *becoming*.

Philosophy, before Hegel, claimed to describe a fixed world in a state of stability where the notion of movement, of becoming, surely was disturbing (already in Greek philosophy), but was not the fundamental problem.

Now Hegel is the philosophy of becoming.

It is the idea of an imperfection of reason which is in the process of moving ahead, of developing.

Schopenhauer links thought to life even more directly, but at the same time he establishes a principle of contemplation, of renunciation, by which one can, so to speak, evade or kill life.

Existentialism *gets bogged down in life*. It is in existence, but it also considers itself to be a vital act (curious thing).

What is the phenomenology of Husserl? It derives from mathematics.

Husserl was a logician and mathematician. His phenomenology is a kind of classification of the facts of consciousness. Now, it is curious that this spiritual algebra of Husserl was used above all by Heidegger for existentialism, which is the complete opposite of Husserlien phenomenology.

These abstract concepts still persist in thought nowadays (that of Aristotle, Catholic, etc.). Now, through a dialectical opposition, [*words missing*] is breaking out against existentialism, in structuralism.

(Gombrowicz finds his bearings, geography of philosophy.)

Structuralism is a difficult thing to define because it originates in different regions of thought. It is both the fruit of mathematical thought, like the linguistic studies of Saussure, and [*sentence incomplete*] and in the sociology of Lévi-Strauss and even [*the text breaks off here*].

About the author

The works of the Polish novelist and playwright Witold Gombrowicz (1904–1969) were deemed scandalous and subversive by Nazis, Stalinists, and the Polish Communist government in turn. Gombrowicz spent twenty-four years in self-imposed exile in Argentina, returned to Europe in 1963, and eventually settled on the French Riviera. His *Cours de philosophie en six heures un quart* began as lectures to his wife, Rita, and his good friend Dominique de Roux. De Roux had edited Gombrowicz's autobiographical *A Kind of Testament,* and the two were so close that Gombrowicz once asked de Roux to get him a gun or some poison so that he could kill himself. De Roux, hoping to take his friend's mind off the heart problems that were eventually to kill him, asked Gombrowicz for lessons in philosophy. According to Rita Gombrowicz, "Dominique understood full well that only philosophy, in this moment of physical decadence, had the power to mobilize his spirit." This first published English translation of *A Guide to Philosophy in Six Hours and Fifteen Minutes* retains the anonymous footnotes and textual gaps of the original French publication.